The Challenger Disaster

Titles in the *American Disasters* series:

The Challenger Disaster
Tragic Space Flight
ISBN 0-7660-1222-0

The Exxon Valdez
Tragic Oil Spill
ISBN 0-7660-1058-9

Fire in Oakland, California
Billion-Dollar Blaze
ISBN 0-7660-1220-4

Hurricane Andrew
Nature's Rage
ISBN 0-7660-1057-0

The L.A. Riots
Rage in the City of Angels
ISBN 0-7660-1219-0

The Mighty Midwest Flood
Raging Rivers
ISBN 0-7660-1221-2

The Oklahoma City Bombing
Terror in the Heartland
ISBN 0-7660-1061-9

Plains Outbreak Tornadoes
Killer Twisters
ISBN 0-7660-1059-7

San Francisco Earthquake, 1989
Death and Destruction
ISBN 0-7660-1060-0

The Siege at Waco
Deadly Inferno
ISBN 0-7660-1218-2

TWA Flight 800
Explosion in Midair
ISBN 0-7660-1217-4

The World Trade Center Bombing
Terror in the Towers
ISBN 0-7660-1056-2

The Challenger Disaster

Tragic Space Flight

Carmen Bredeson

AMERICAN DISASTERS

Enslow Publishers, Inc.

40 Industrial Road   PO Box 38
Box 398   Aldershot
Berkeley Heights, NJ 07922 Hants GU12 6BP
USA   UK

http://www.enslow.com

Copyright © 1999 by Carmen Bredeson

B+T 5|1|01 18.95Z

All rights reserved.

Library of Congress Cataloging-in-Publication Data

Bredeson, Carmen.
    The Challenger disaster : tragic space flight / Carmen Bredeson.
        p. cm. — (American disasters)
    Includes bibliographical references and index.
    Summary: Describes the events surrounding the explosion of the
Challenger shuttle in 1986, the investigation of this disaster, and
the seven astronauts who died.
    ISBN 0-7660-1222-0
    1. Space vehicle accidents—United States—Juvenile literature.
    2. Challenger (Spacecraft)—Juvenile literature. [1. Challenger
(Spacecraft)—Accidents. 2. Space shuttles—Accidents.] I. Title.
II. Series.
TL867.B74   1999
363.12'465—dc21   98-46685
                                                            CIP
                                                            AC

Printed in the United States of America

10 9 8 7 6 5 4 3 2 1

To Our Readers:
All Internet addresses in this book were active and appropriate when we went to press.
Any comments or suggestions can be sent by e-mail to Comments@enslow.com or to
the address on the back cover.

Photo Credits: AP/Wide World Photos, pp. 6, 8, 11, 14, 15, 32, 35; Grace
Corrigan, p. 40; NASA, pp. 1, 9, 12, 18, 19, 20, 23, 24, 25, 26, 27, 29, 34, 36, 41.

Cover Photo: AP/Wide World Photos.

Contents

1 January 28, 1986 7

2 Picking Up the Pieces 13

3 Flight 51-L 22

4 Investigation 31

5 Aftermath 38

Glossary 43

Chapter Notes 44

Further Reading 46

Internet Sites 47

Index 48

January 28, 1986

Four . . . three . . . two . . . one . . . And liftoff. Liftoff of the twenty-fifth space shuttle mission. And it has cleared the tower."[1] Trailing smoke and flames, the space shuttle *Challenger* began rising toward the bright blue sky over the Kennedy Space Center in Cape Canaveral, Florida. On board were astronauts Gregory Jarvis, Christa McAuliffe, Ronald McNair, Ellison Onizuka, Judith Resnik, Richard Scobee, and Michael Smith. It was 11:38 A.M. on the morning of Tuesday, January 28, 1986.

In the viewing stands four miles from launchpad 39-B, sixteen third-grade students clapped and yelled. They were classmates of Scott McAuliffe whose mother, Christa, was on board the *Challenger*. Keeping an eye on the wiggling children were Christa's parents, Grace and Ed Corrigan. Also in the crowded viewing stands were hundreds of relatives and friends of the other *Challenger* crew members.

Some of the astronauts' relatives were watching the launch from the rooftop of a nearby National Aeronautics and Space Administration (NASA) building. Among them

S cott McAuliffe (center) poses with two of his classmates as he awaits the liftoff of his mother's space mission.

was the twenty-five-year-old daughter of Dick Scobee, commander of the *Challenger*. Kathie Scobee Fulgham held her baby son, Justin, tightly in her arms as the shuttle carrying her father was about to roar into space. Standing near her was Jane Smith, wife of Mike Smith, the shuttle's pilot. The Smiths' three children were close by their mother's side.

All along roads and beaches near the Kennedy Space Center, people stopped to watch the launch of Space Shuttle Mission 51-L. Heads turned to look at the sky as noise from the rockets filled the air. Soon a giant roaring sound vibrated the air around all of the onlookers. The sound got bigger and louder as the shuttle slowly lifted from the launchpad. Cheers and whistles could barely be heard over the deafening roar.

All across America schoolchildren were allowed to watch television so they, too, could see the *Challenger* launch. There was a great deal of interest in the mission, since it carried Christa McAuliffe, the first schoolteacher chosen to fly aboard a space shuttle. At Concord High School in New Hampshire, where McAuliffe taught social studies, the students proudly blew party horns as the shuttle lifted off. They cheered their teacher, who was making history.

As soon as the *Challenger* cleared the control tower, control of the mission passed from the Kennedy Space Center to Mission Control in Houston, Texas. Dick Scobee and Mike Smith, as the shuttle's commander and pilot, were then in direct communication with Richard Covey at Mission Control in Houston. Just after takeoff (T), their voices could be heard saying:

T plus 0:01 (seconds after takeoff) Smith: Here we go![2]

T plus 0:16 Scobee: Houston, we have roll program.[3]

At this point, the shuttle turned over on its back to be in the correct position to go into orbit around the earth.

T plus 0:28 Smith: There's 10,000 feet and Mach point five.

T plus 0:35 Scobee: Point nine.

T plus 0:41 Scobee: Going through 19,000 feet.

T plus 0:67 Covey: Go at throttle up.

T plus 0:70 Scobee: Roger, go at throttle up.

T plus 0:73 Smith: Uhh . . . oh![4]

The *Challenger* had reached an altitude of 50,800 feet and was traveling at a

*A*t 50,800 feet, *Challenger* suddenly exploded. Bits of debris from the shuttle shot downward, leaving smoke trails throughout the sky.

speed of 2,900 feet per second when suddenly it exploded in a huge blaze of fire, smoke, and debris. Its two solid rocket boosters broke free of the main part of the shuttle and belched smoke and fire as they plunged rapidly back down toward the Atlantic Ocean. Then the *Challenger*'s nose pitched up, and its wings and rear fuselage, or cargo bay, broke off. A huge fireball and clouds of smoke filled the sky over Cape Canaveral.

Those watching from the ground were not sure what they were seeing, but slowly they began to realize that something terrible was happening. Jane Smith said, "They're gone." Her son asked, "What do you mean, Mom?" She replied, "They're lost."[5] Another one of Mike Smith's children cried out, "Daddy! Daddy! I want you. Daddy! You promised nothing would happen."[6] Christa McAuliffe's dad, Ed Corrigan, reached out to put an arm around his wife's shoulder. Then, when they saw the horrified looks on the adult faces around them, Scott McAuliffe's classmates began to cry. Similarly, complete strangers who had stopped along the roadways to witness this great national event looked at the smoke filling the sky and wept.

As the crowd watched the fireball above them, Steve Nesbitt, the Mission Control commentator, continued eerily to broadcast over the loudspeakers: "We're at a minute 15 seconds, velocity 2,900 feet per second, altitude 9 nautical miles, range distance 7 nautical miles." Then a long silence followed and Nesbitt said, "Flight controllers are looking very carefully at the situation.

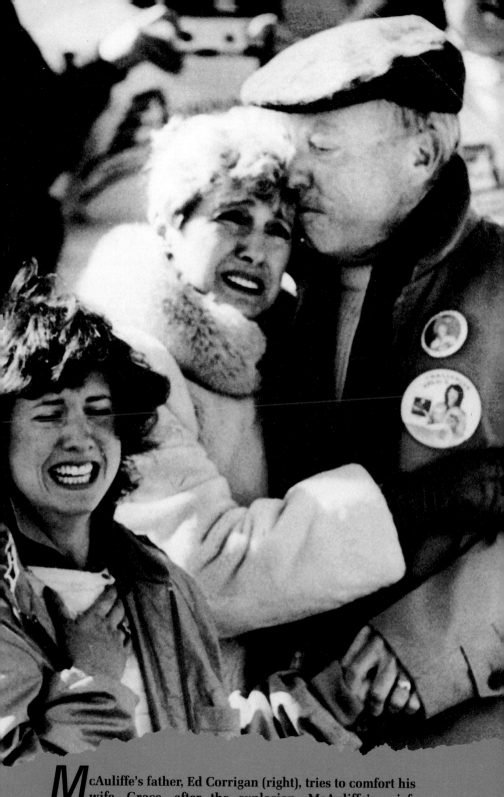

McAuliffe's father, Ed Corrigan (right), tries to comfort his wife, Grace, after the explosion. McAuliffe's grief-stricken sister, Betsy, places her hand over her heart.

Obviously we have had a major malfunction. We have no downlink."[7] That meant there were no longer any radio signals coming from *Challenger*. A few minutes later, Nesbitt confirmed what everyone already knew: "We have a report from the flight dynamics officer that the vehicle has exploded."[8]

Gone in an instant were the seven brave Americans on board: Gregory Jarvis, age 41; Christa McAuliffe, 37; Ronald McNair, 35; Ellison Onizuka, 39; Judith Resnik, 36; Richard Scobee, 46; and Michael Smith, 40.

*C*louds of smoke fill the sky over Cape Canaveral shortly after the *Challenger* explodes.

CHAPTER 2

Picking Up the Pieces

Immediately after the explosion, the astronauts' families were rushed onto buses and driven to the crew's quarters. Christa McAuliffe's husband, Steve, and their children sat in Christa's dorm room. Her tennis shoes were still on the floor, next to the bed. He said, "This is not how it's supposed to be."[1] In another room, Ronald McNair's wife, Cheryl, tried to assure her children that "we wouldn't be able to see Daddy anymore, physically, but that we would be able to feel him, spiritually."[2]

In about an hour, as soon as debris from the *Challenger* explosion stopped raining down from the sky, rescue planes were sent to the area. On board were paramedics who parachuted into the ocean to search for survivors. No one expected to find any of the astronauts alive, but a rescue effort was launched just to be sure. At 4:30 P.M. on the afternoon of the explosion, NASA held a press conference and reported that there was no evidence that any of the *Challenger* crew members had survived the blast and were floating, freely, in the sea.

In Washington, D.C., President Ronald Reagan was getting ready to give the State of the Union address to the nation later that day, when he heard about the *Challenger* disaster. Quickly, the president canceled his speech. He decided to use the scheduled television time to talk about the tragedy instead. He said,

And I want to say something to the schoolchildren of America who were watching the live coverage of the shuttle's takeoff. I know it is hard to understand, that sometimes painful things like this happen. It's all part of the process of exploration and discovery. It's all part of taking a chance and expanding man's horizons. The future doesn't belong to the fainthearted; it belongs to the brave. The *Challenger* crew was pulling us into the future, and we'll continue to follow them.[3]

*F*ollowing the *Challenger* disaster, President Ronald Reagan speaks to the nation, praising the crew's bravery.

On the morning after the explosion, Navy and Coast Guard ships began searching for wreckage in the Atlantic Ocean. Air Force planes flew overhead, trying to spot floating debris for the ships to collect. During the next two days, several tons of wreckage were picked out of the water. Papers belonging to Christa McAuliffe were found floating

A section of the *Challenger*'s tiled fuselage floats in the Atlantic Ocean off the coast of Florida.

in the sea. Written on them were lessons that she had planned to teach from space. The lessons were to be on the effects of microgravity and how spaceflight benefits people on earth. After the surface wreckage was picked up, the search became much more difficult. The rest of the *Challenger*, including the crew's cabin, had sunk to the bottom of the ocean.

Gradually, over the next few days, families of the *Challenger* crew left the Kennedy Space Center and returned to their homes. An astronaut was assigned to each family to help them handle the reporters, insurance forms, mail, and telephone calls that were about to overwhelm them. A memorial service was scheduled for Friday, January 31, 1986, at the Johnson Space Center in Houston, where the astronauts had trained.

On the morning of the memorial service, President and Nancy Reagan met privately with the crew's family members in a NASA classroom. After hugging each one, Reagan said, "We'll all go out together in a few minutes. I wish there was something I could say to make it easier, but there just aren't any words."[4] Then they all left the building to join ten thousand NASA employees, friends, and relatives who were gathered together in a grassy area in between several buildings. An Air Force band played hymns while some participants cried and others waved small American flags.

Addressing the gathering, President Reagan said,

> The future is not free; the story of all human progress is one of a struggle against all odds. We learned again that this America was built on heroism and noble sacrifice. It was built by men and women like our seven star voyagers, who answered a call beyond duty. . . . Dick, Mike, Judy, El, Ron, Greg, and Christa—your families and your country mourn your passing. We bid you goodbye, but we will never forget you.[5]

At the end of the thirty-minute ceremony, four T-38 jets flew overhead in the missing-man formation. They would have made the shape of a perfect V except that the fifth plane was not there. The missing plane symbolized the missing astronauts. While the band played "God Bless America," the president and Mrs. Reagan went down the line of family members again. They offered words of sympathy, shook hands, and hugged the crying children.

In memory of the *Challenger* crew, flags all over the

United States were lowered to half-staff, and signs appeared in many towns that said, "We salute our heroes. God bless them all."[6] Floodlights that normally light up the Empire State Building in New York City were turned off in memory of the astronauts. On the night of January 31, along the Florida coast, more than twenty thousand people pointed flashlights at the sky in a prearranged tribute to their heroes.

On February 3, Ronald Reagan signed Executive Order 12546. It created the Presidential Committee on the Space Shuttle *Challenger* Accident. The committee would be headed by William Rogers, former secretary of state under President Nixon. Also among those investigating the accident would be former astronauts Neil Armstrong and Sally Ride. During the two months that the commission reviewed flight data and examined videos of the seventy-three-second *Challenger* flight, salvage efforts continued in the Atlantic Ocean. From the start of the investigation, evidence pointed to the right solid rocket booster as a source of the explosion.

Ships using radar and sonar devices scanned the ocean floor, looking for pieces of debris that might be part of the *Challenger.* Divers and remote-controlled submarines were sent underwater to examine suspicious areas. When pieces of wreckage were found, cables were attached to them, and they were then hauled to the surface and identified. On February 16, a memo was issued stating, "The four-man submarine dispatched yesterday has found

*T*he U.S.S. *Preserver* helped collect debris from the explosion, which would be analyzed to try and find out what went wrong.

what is believed to be components of the right-hand solid rocket booster from the Space Shuttle *Challenger*."[7]

High winds and rough seas prevented further searches during the first few days in March. Then, on March 8, divers found and identified the *Challenger* crew cabin, which was resting on the sand, one hundred feet down. All seven astronauts were still strapped to their seats inside the cabin. Divers placed the remains of the astronauts in containers and brought them to the surface. They were then taken to a hangar, located at Cape Canaveral, for identification and examination.

Dr. Joseph Kerwin, director of life sciences at the Johnson Space Center and a former astronaut, directed the further investigation into the deaths of the *Challenger* crew. In his report to the commission, Dr. Kerwin said that some of the crew had probably survived the explosion that occurred seventy-three seconds into the flight. He based his opinion on the fact that four emergency oxygen packs had been recovered and three of them had been activated. The oxygen did not come on automatically but had to be turned on manually. At least three of

*A*fter they were recovered from the Atlantic Ocean, pieces of wreckage from the *Challenger* were reassembled.

the astronauts had survived the blast and turned on their emergency oxygen supply, which would last for six minutes. The oxygen in Mike Smith's pack was three-quarters gone when it was recovered. Dick Scobee's air pack had not been turned on.

Dr. Kerwin could not determine the exact cause of death for the crew. He said that they might have died of decompression if the cabin had lost pressure during the breakup of the fuselage. He explained that after the explosion, the crew's cabin continued to go upward for a few seconds before heading back down toward the ocean. The fall toward the water took nearly three minutes, ending

*T*he remains of the *Challenger* crew were moved from the Kennedy Space Center in Florida to the Dover Air Force Base in Delaware.

when the cabin hit the water at two hundred miles per hour. Anyone still alive inside the *Challenger* would have died from the force of the impact.

After the crew's remains had been examined, they were taken to Dover Air Force Base in Delaware and released to the families for burial. Dick Scobee and Michael Smith were buried at Arlington National Cemetery in Washington, D.C. Ellison Onizuka was buried in Hawaii, Judith Resnik in Ohio, Ronald McNair in South Carolina, and Christa McAuliffe in New Hampshire. The remains of Gregory Jarvis were cremated, and his ashes were sprinkled into the Pacific Ocean off the coast of California.

What had begun as a great adventure ended as a terrible tragedy. But the seven astronauts who lost their lives aboard the space shuttle *Challenger* will always be remembered as heroes.

CHAPTER 3

Flight 51-L

Space shuttle astronauts are divided into three basic categories: the flight crew, mission specialists, and payload specialists. The flight crew is made up of the commander and the pilot. Mission specialists operate the shuttle's mechanical systems, such as the robot arm. They also launch satellites and perform space walks. Payload specialists carry out the scientific experiments that are a part of each shuttle flight.

Shuttle commander Dick Scobee, father of two children and a former enlisted Air Force mechanic, had attended night school to earn an aerospace engineering degree, which qualified him to become an officer and a pilot. June Scobee, his wife, related, "Our family always tried to be together for dinner, and Dick listened as closely to our daily adventures as we did to his."[1] When describing his work as an astronaut, Dick Scobee joked, "You know, it's a real crime to be paid for a job that I have so much fun doing."[2]

Shuttle pilot Mike Smith, father of three children, was a Navy captain and a former Vietnam combat pilot. According to his wife, Jane, "Mike's family was always first in his heart despite his busy schedule. . . ." She added, ". . . whenever our children were away, Mike helped them maintain their lawn-mowing business in Houston. Our friends used to say, 'It's so funny to look out and see an astronaut mowing our lawn,'"[3] After his brother's death, Pat Smith said, "I hope everybody realizes that Mike was doing just exactly what he wanted to do."[4]

Judith Resnik, Mission Specialist 1, was one of the first six women selected for NASA astronaut training and

*C*ommander Dick Scobee attended night school to earn his degree in aerospace engineering.

*S*huttle pilot Mike Smith was a Vietnam veteran and the father of three.

J udith Resnik, the second American woman in space, was Mission Specialist 1.

E llison Onizuka, father of two and the first Asian American to fly in space, was Mission Specialist 2.

the second American woman to fly in space. She had a doctorate in electrical engineering and was a classical pianist and a gourmet cook. Her father, Marvin Resnik, said that "Judith once wrote a letter to a friend in which she told her that nothing is obtained by wishing for it, that hard work and perseverance are necessary for success. And that's the way she lived her life, whether in high school, college, or NASA."[5] On the day of the *Challenger* flight, Judith Resnik carried with her a signet ring that belonged to her nephew and a heart-shaped locket belonging to her niece.

Ellison Onizuka, Mission Specialist 2, father of two

children, was an Air Force lieutenant colonel and the first Asian-American astronaut to fly in space. As a child growing up in Hawaii, Onizuka may have worked in the coffee fields, but he had his mind on the stars. He often visited the telescope at the Bishop Museum in Honolulu to study the sky. His seventy-two-year-old grandmother, Matsue Onizuka, remembered, "Ellison always had it in his mind to become an astronaut but was too embarrassed to tell anyone. When he was growing up there were no Asian astronauts, no black astronauts, just white ones. His dream seemed too big."[6]

Ronald McNair, Mission Specialist 3, father of two children, had a doctorate in physics and a fifth-degree black belt in karate and was the second African American to fly in space. Growing up in the rural South, McNair learned to pick tobacco to earn money. His first-grade teacher, Irene Jones, remembered that while out at recess, Ronald would "lie flat on his back, stare up at the sky and just smile."[7] McNair once told a group of students, "The true courage of space flight is not sitting aboard 6 million pounds of fire and thunder as one rockets away from this planet. True courage comes in

Ronald McNair, Mission Specialist 3, was the second African American in space.

*G*regory Jarvis beat out six hundred other employees of the Hughes Aircraft Corporation to join the *Challenger*'s crew as Payload Specialist 1.

enduring . . . persevering, the preparation and believing in oneself."[8]

Gregory Jarvis, Payload Specialist 1, was an engineer for the Hughes Aircraft Corporation in California. When NASA asked Hughes to recommend an employee to fly aboard the shuttle, six hundred Hughes employees applied. Jarvis got the job. He was a civilian astronaut who planned to test a device for mixing rocket fuel in an environment that was weightless. Jarvis had been attending night school in Los Angeles and had completed the classwork necessary for a master's degree in management science. The degree was going to be awarded to him in a ceremony aboard *Challenger*. On the day before the flight, Jarvis talked about NASA: "For any contingency, they know what to do. So I feel very, very comfortable. I'm excited, but not nervous."[9]

Christa McAuliffe, Payload Specialist 2, was the mother of two children, and because she was the first civilian teacher chosen to fly aboard the space shuttle, she was the darling of the media and, therefore, of the nation. During the mission, McAuliffe, a social studies teacher, was scheduled to teach two classes that would be broadcast over television to schools across America. Jennifer LaPurre, one of her former students from Concord High School, remembered that McAuliffe used to say, "Any dream can come true if you have the courage and work at it."[10] After she joined the astronaut program, Christa McAuliffe explained, "What are we doing here? We're reaching for the stars."[11]

*C*hrista McAuliffe, Payload Specialist 2, was a social studies teacher. She had planned to teach two classes from space.

On the morning of January 28, 1986, these seven people arrived at the launchpad at a little after 8:00 A.M. By 8:36 the astronauts were strapped into their seats and ready for the scheduled 9:38 launch. Temperatures in Florida had fallen to record lows the night before, and long icicles covered the launch tower. Christa McAuliffe's mother, Grace Corrigan, in the viewing stands waiting to watch her daughter soar into space, remembered that "It was cold, cold, cold. Groups of people were awaiting liftoff huddled together, stamping their feet and wrapping their arms around themselves trying to keep warm. Everyone wondered why a liftoff should be scheduled in such freezing weather."[12]

Because of the unusually low temperatures, liftoff was delayed to allow time for some of the ice on the launch tower to melt. Inside the shuttle, the astronauts went through routine communications drills with astronaut support team member Manley Carter to make sure their radios were working properly.

Carter: Good morning, Judy.

Resnik: Cowabunga.

Carter: Heyyy!

Scobee: Loud and clear, there, Judy.

Carter: Okay, Christa, you oughta be able to hear me.

McAuliffe: Real fine.

Carter: Good morning, Greg.

Jarvis: Good morning, Billy Bob. How are you?

Carter: Fine. And you?

Jarvis: Fannnnntastic![13]

After Carter checked each astronaut's radio, the decision to launch was finally made. The temperature had risen to just above freezing, and some of the ice on the launchpad was melting. Inside the crew cabin, the astronauts heard the welcome words:

Launch Control Center: We're planning to come out of this hold on time.

Scobee: All riiight. Roger, go ahead. That's great.[14]

The voice of Hugh Harris, a NASA commentator, could be heard over the loudspeakers at the Kennedy Space Center and in the viewing stands:

Harris: One minute away from picking up the count for the final nine minutes in the countdown.

*B*ecause of the record low temperatures in Florida the night before, icicles covered the launch tower on the morning of *Challenger*'s liftoff.

Harris: T minus 8 minutes 30 seconds and counting. All the flight recorders are turned on.

Harris: T minus 7 minutes 30 seconds, and the ground launch sequencer has started retracting the orbiter crew access arm.[15]

The count continued until only a minute remained until liftoff. Inside the shuttle, Dick Scobee and Mike Smith were busy with launch procedures.

T minus 0:59 Scobee: One minute downstairs.

T minus 0:53 Smith: Alarm looks good.

T minus 0:42 Scobee: OK.

T minus 0:30 Scobee: Thirty seconds down there.

T minus 0:15 Scobee: Fifteen.

T minus 0:06 Scobee: There they go, guys [the main engines started firing].

T minus 0:06 Resnik: All right.

T plus 0:01 Smith: Here we go![16]

First, there was triumph, as the mighty vehicle lifted off. Then, to the horror of the nation, the space shuttle exploded in a giant fireball seventy-three seconds later. The loss of *Challenger* and its seven astronauts was the worst disaster in NASA's history. In the months after the tragedy, investigators spent countless hours trying to pinpoint the exact cause of the explosion.

CHAPTER 4

Investigation

As wreckage from the *Challenger* was brought ashore, the pieces were taken to a hangar and fitted together. A few days after the crew compartment was found on March 8, divers located five computers and three flight recorders. Then on March 19, a three thousand-pound section of the right solid rocket booster was found. By early April, another piece of the right booster was found. In it had been burned a twenty-eight by fifteen-inch hole.

Investigators continued to focus on the right solid rocket booster as the source of the explosion. Videotapes taken by one of the cameras at the Kennedy Space Center showed a sequence of events that could not be seen by ground controllers or spectators. By examining the films, computer programs, and the pieces of recovered wreckage very carefully, a terrible picture began to emerge.

Captured on film at just .445 seconds after ignition, a puff of dark smoke appeared close to a joint on the right booster. By 2.147 seconds into the flight, there was smoke

Two views of the shuttle show a dark patch of smoke (in white circles) emerging between the left solid rocket booster and the bottom of *Challenger*'s external tank. The left-hand photo was taken at 11:38.01810 A.M.; the right-hand photo was taken only .00033 seconds later.

streaming across half the booster. The shuttle then appeared to operate smoothly for the next forty-five seconds. Smoke appeared again at 58.774 seconds, just above one of the places where the right booster was attached to the shuttle. By 59.249 seconds, a seal had cracked open, spewing forth a stream of hot gasses onto the outside of the booster.

Investigators theorized that as the right booster lost fuel, pressure inside it started to fall until it no longer matched the pressure in the left solid rocket booster. Computers detected the difference at 60.164 seconds and gave commands to correct the imbalance at 62.434 seconds. At 67.684 seconds, sensors detected a pressure problem in the liquid oxygen line. Then a flash appeared at 73.175 seconds into the flight, followed by a fireball showing on the videotape at 73.621 seconds after liftoff. The sound of an explosion could be heard on a voice tape at 73:534 seconds. There were no more transmissions from *Challenger*.[1]

The committee investigating the *Challenger* disaster met for two months. During that time they collected one hundred twenty-two thousand pages of information. In June 1986, they published their findings in a five-volume report. Specifically, the accident was blamed on the failure of an O-ring on the right solid rocket booster. The O-ring, a relatively simple nine hundred-dollar part, was like a huge rubber band that sealed two sections of the booster tightly together. Cold weather on the night before the launch had made the O-ring stiff and brittle, so that it failed to seal properly.

In the boosters, solid fuel burns at a very high temperature. Smoke and fire are forced out of the tail of the rocket under tremendous pressure. This force is what lifts the rockets and orbiter into the sky. The brittle O-ring allowed fire to leak out of the side of the rocket casing. The stream of fire was pointed right at a support that

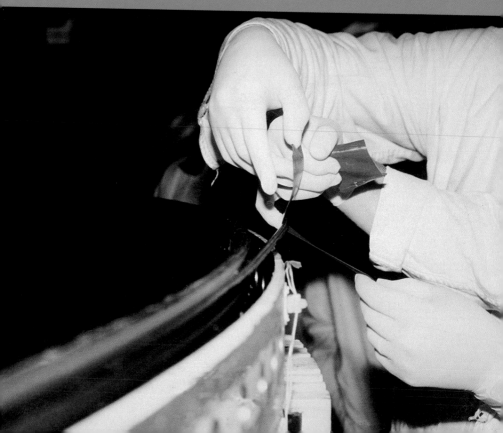

In this photo, an O-ring is being studied. The safety of the O-rings was one of the issues questioned during the *Challenger* investigation.

attached the booster to the shuttle. The fire acted like a blowtorch and cut the support in half. With the support gone, the booster broke free and slammed into the liquid fuel tank. The impact created a giant explosion and fireball, which tore the shuttle apart.

Eventually, the investigating committee found that both NASA and Morton Thiokol, the company that made the O-rings, were at fault. Engineers at Thiokol had warned NASA that the O-rings could have problems if the temperature dipped too low. NASA ignored their warning and decided to

A NASA official holds a mock-up of the *Challenger's* O-ring seal. Due to the cold weather, the shuttle's O-ring failed to seal properly.

launch *Challenger* in near-freezing temperatures anyway. The mission had been postponed three times already, and mission controllers were eager to get it off the ground. There had already been twenty-three successful shuttle flights. Perhaps the missions had become so routine and dependable to NASA that some people had forgotten about the ever-present dangers of spaceflight.

As a result of the *Challenger* explosion, shuttle launches were discontinued for nearly three years. During that time, more than three hundred changes were made in the space shuttle system. Astronauts are now supplied with parachutes and more convenient emergency oxygen supplies. The crew compartment hatches can be opened from the inside, and astronauts routinely practice evacuation procedures. Today, if a problem should occur shortly after liftoff, shuttle crews have a better chance of surviving.

*A*ll astronaut candidates, like Dr. Ellen Ochoa, above, participate in survival training sessions, which ensure them a better chance of surviving an emergency.

Discovery was the first shuttle to fly after the *Challenger* disaster. It lifted off from Pad 39 B at the Kennedy Space Center on September 29, 1988. As *Discovery* rose into the sky, employees at the Johnson Space Center in Houston clapped and yelled, "Go, baby, go." One of the engineers watching the launch said, "I think everybody was tense. There was a lot of relief after seventy-three seconds passed by. I was relieved even more after the two solid rocket boosters separated."[2] Dozens of other successful shuttle missions have flown in the years since the tragic flight of *Challenger*. While the space program has been getting on with the business of exploration, the families of the *Challenger* crew have also moved forward.

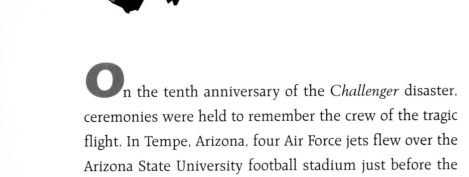

CHAPTER 5

Aftermath

On the tenth anniversary of the *Challenger* disaster, ceremonies were held to remember the crew of the tragic flight. In Tempe, Arizona, four Air Force jets flew over the Arizona State University football stadium just before the start of the Super Bowl. One of the airplanes was flown by Captain Rich Scobee, son of *Challenger* pilot Dick Scobee. Four hundred people also gathered at the Kennedy Space Center on January 28, 1996. After they observed seventy-three seconds of silence, four T-38 jets flew overhead in the missing-man formation.

When a group of college students were asked where they were when *Challenger* exploded, many of them vividly remembered the event that had happened ten years earlier. Scott Shogan recalled that he ". . . was home from school sick. I was flipping through the channels and I saw it right after it happened." Nellie Peretsian said, "I was in the fifth grade and eating lunch in our school's cafeteria. And our music teacher started crying. She had a small radio next to her and the whole cafeteria fell silent. From the radio we all listened to the newscasters and found out what happened. There were five hundred kids in there, and we were all silent."[1]

Grace Corrigan also recalls that terrible day in 1986 when her daughter, Christa McAuliffe, lost her life. As Grace and her husband, Ed, were waiting for liftoff in the freezing cold, he told her, "I'd take her off that thing if I could get out there. Things don't seem to be going the way we thought they would." Grace answered, "Even if you could, she wouldn't come."[2] Later, Grace said that "Christa always accomplished everything that she was capable of accomplishing. She extended her own limitations."[3] In memory of her daughter, Grace Corrigan wrote a book called *A Journal for Christa* in 1993.

June Scobee, wife of commander Dick Scobee, also recalled the day of the disaster. "We stood there in stunned silence. Our eyes spoke volumes, but there were no words."[4] However, instead of wallowing in sorrow, Scobee got her life moving again and became the founding director of the Challenger Center for Space Exploration. The nonprofit organization has helped establish Challenger Learning Centers in more than thirty cities in the United States and Canada. Fourteen more centers are scheduled to open during the next two years, including one in England. Many of the *Challenger* family members work to promote these centers.

Each has two rooms equipped with computers. In one room, there is a simulation, or mock-up, of the space

*T*his statue by artist W.D. Bill Hopin, commemorating Christa McAuliffe, was made from pennies that were sent in by students all over the country, then melted down. It resides in the rose garden of the Sunrise Museum in Charleston, West Virginia.

shuttle and in the other, a simulation of mission control. Classes visiting the center work in teams to solve problems that might really occur during a mission. The students work as astronauts, communicators, engineers, scientists, and mission controllers. There are costumes and props to make the activities more realistic. The goal of the centers is to encourage student interest in technology, science, math, and space exploration.

Dick Scobee's grandson, Justin, is a frequent visitor to the Challenger Center in Houston. He was the infant that Kathie Scobee Fulgham had held while she watched her father lift off aboard *Challenger* in 1986. During a visit to the center, Justin said, "I like the shuttle simulator best. It would be fun in space. You can float because it's zero g [zero gravity]. I would like to become an astronaut."[5]

*B*arbara Morgan (right), backup for Christa McAuliffe (left) on the *Challenger* mission, kept pursuing her own dream of spaceflight.

When Christa McAuliffe trained at NASA for her flight aboard *Challenger*, a backup teacher trained by her side. Each astronaut assigned to a flight has a backup who can act as a replacement in an emergency. In case McAuliffe had been unable to go on the mission, Barbara Morgan, also a civilian schoolteacher, would have flown in her place. There had not been another civilian teacher assigned to a shuttle mission since 1986, but Morgan continued to get a flight physical every year just in case the program was started again. Finally, her perseverance paid off.

In January 1998, NASA announced that Barbara Morgan would be among the new class of astronaut trainees. The third-grade teacher from Idaho expressed many people's feelings about the *Challenger* disaster when she said, "What happened was horrible, and you can't ever erase that. But our job as teachers is to help kids reach their potential. *Challenger* reminds us that we should never quit reaching for the stars."[6]

Glossary

altitude—The height of an object above a surface.

booster—The part of the shuttle that provides thrust for a launch.

debris—The remains of something that has been destroyed.

decompression—A condition caused by exposure to rapidly lowered air pressure.

downlink—A transmission from a spacecraft.

fuselage—The exterior and interior central portions of an aircraft designed to house the crew, passengers, and cargo.

Mach—A number that represents the ratio of the speed of a spacecraft to the speed of sound.

malfunction—Something not functioning or operating correctly.

Mission Control—The group of NASA scientists and experts assigned to monitoring a spaceflight.

orbit—A path around a heavenly body, in this case a spacecraft's path around such a body.

O-ring—A ring of synthetic rubber used to make a joint fluid-tight.

Chapter 1. January 28, 1986

1. Ed Magnuson, "They Slipped the Surly Bonds of Earth to Touch the Face of God," *Time*, February 10, 1986, p. 27.
2. Richard Lewis, *Challenger: The Final Voyage* (New York: Columbia University Press, 1988), p. 15.
3. Magnuson, p. 27.
4. Lewis, p. 25.
5. Claudia Dowling, "Ten Years Ago, Seven Brave Americans Died as They Reached for the Stars," *Life*, February 1996, p. 39+.
6. Lewis, p. 22.
7. Carlos Byars, "Challenger Explodes," *Houston Chronicle*, January 28, 1986, p. A1.
8. Magnuson, p. 28.

Chapter 2. Picking Up the Pieces

1. Claudia Dowling, "Ten Years Ago, Seven Brave Americans Died as They Reached for the Stars," *Life*, February 1996, p. 39.
2. Ibid., p. 39+.
3. "President Ronald Reagan's Speech on the Challenger Disaster," *Essential Documents in American History*, 1977, p. 1.
4. Ed Magnuson, "They Slipped the Surly Bonds of Earth to Touch the Face of God," *Time*, February 10, 1986, p. 31.
5. Ibid., p. 31.
6. Ibid., pp. 24–25.
7. Richard Lewis, *Challenger: The Final Voyage* (New York: Columbia University Press, 1988), p. 156.

Chapter 3. Flight 51-L

1. "Tribute," *People*, December 22–29, 1986, p. 120.
2. Paul Gray, "Seven Who Flew for All of Us," *Time*, February 10, 1986, p. 33.
3. "Tribute," p. 119.
4. Gray, p. 34.
5. "Tribute," p. 123.
6. Gray, p. 35.
7. Ibid., p. 34.
8. Ibid., p. 34.

9. Ibid., p. 35.

10. Ron Arias, "A Lesson in Uncommon Valor," *People*, February 10, 1986, p. 37.

11. Gray, p. 32.

12. Grace Corrigan, *A Journal For Christa* (Lincoln: University of Nebraska Press, 1993), p. 3.

13. Richard Lewis, *Challenger: The Final Voyage* (New York: Columbia University Press, 1988), p. 11.

14. Ibid., p. 12.

15. Ibid., p. 14.

16. Ibid., p. 15.

Chapter 4. Investigation

1. Wayne Biddle, "What Destroyed Challenger?" *Discover*, April 1986, p. 42.

2. Mark Carreau, "U.S. Soars Back Into Space," *Houston Chronicle*, September 29, 1988, p. A1.

Chapter 5. Aftermath

1. "Students Remember Sadness After Challenger Explosion," <http://grizzly.umt.edu> (March 12, 1998).

2. Grace Corrigan, *A Journal for Christa* (Lincoln: University of Nebraska Press, 1993), p. 4.

3. Ibid., p. xii.

4. Fred Bruning, "The Challenger Explosion," *Newsday*, January 28, 1996, p. A7.

5. Claudia Dowling, "Ten Years Ago, Seven Brave Americans Died as They Reached for the Stars," *Life*, February 1996, p. 39+.

6. Ibid., p. 39.

Further Reading

Bernstein, Joanne. *Judith Resnik: Challenger Astronaut.* New York: Lodestar Books, 1990.

Bredeson, Carmen. *Gus Grissom: A Space Biography.* Springfield, N. J.: Enslow Publishers, Inc., 1998.

———. *Shannon Lucid: Space Ambassador.* Brookfield, Conn.: Millbrook Press, 1998.

Cole, Michael D. *Challenger: America's Space Tragedy.* Springfield, N.J.: Enslow Publishers, Inc., 1995.

Corrigan, Grace. *A Journal for Christa.* Lincoln: University of Nebraska Press, 1993.

Lampton, Christopher. *Undersea Archaeology.* New York: Franklin Watts, 1988.

Lewis, Richard. *Challenger: The Final Voyage.* New York: Columbia University Press, 1988.

Rodgers, June Scobee. *Silver Linings.* Macon, Georgia: Peake Road, 1995.

Shaw, Dena. *Ronald McNair.* New York: Chelsea House, 1994.

Stern, Alan. *The U.S. Space Program After Challenger.* New York: Franklin Watts, 1987.

Internet Sites

Challenger Center OnLine
<http://www.challenger.org>

Federation of American Scientists (FAS) Space
Policy Project—51-L: The Challenger Accident
<http://www.fas.org/spp/51L.html>

Jet Propulsion Laboratory
<http://www.jpl.nasa.gov/>

Kennedy Space Center
<http://www.ksc.nasa.gov/ksc.html>

NASA: Space Link
<http://spacelink.msfc.nasa.gov/home.index.html>

A

Arlington National Cemetery, 21
Armstrong, Neil, 17

C

Cape Canaveral, Florida, 7, 10, 18
Carter, Manley, 28
Challenger Center for Space
    Exploration, 39–41
cold weather, 27–28, *29*, 33–34,
    35
Concord High School, 8–9, 27
Corrigan, Ed, 7, 10, *11*, 39
Corrigan, Grace, 7, *11*, 27, 39
countdown, 7, 28, 30
Covey, Richard, 9
crew cabin, 15, 18, 20–21, 28, 31

D

Discovery, 37
Dover Air Force Base, 20, 21

E

emergency oxygen packs, 19, 36
external liquid fuel tank, *32*, 35

F

flight crew, 22
Fulgham, Justin, 8, 40–41
Fulgham, Kathie Scobee, 8, 41

H

Harris, Hugh, 28, 30
Hughes Aircraft Corporation, 26

J

Jarvis, Gregory, 7, 12, 21, *26*, 28
Johnson Space Center, 15–16,
    18, 37

K

Kennedy Space Center, 7, 8, 9,
    15, 28, 31, 37, 38
Kerwin, Joseph, 18–20

L

liftoff, 7, 8–9, 27, 28, 30, 33, 36,
    37, 39, 41

M

McAuliffe, Christa, 7, 8–9, 10,
    12, 13, 14–15, 21, 26–27, 28,
    39, *40*, 41, 42
McAuliffe, Scott, 7, *8*, 10
McAuliffe, Steve, 13
McNair, Cheryl, 13
McNair, Ronald, 7, 12, 13, 21, *25*
missing-man formation, 16, 38
Mission Control, 9, 10, 39
mission specialists, 22
Morgan, Barbara, *41*, 42
Morton Thiokol, 35

N

National Aeronautics and Space
    Administration (NASA), 7,
    13, 16, 23, 24, 26, 28, 30, 35,
    41, 42
Nesbitt, Steve, 10, 12

O

Ochoa, Ellen, *36*
Onizuka, Ellison, 7, 12, 21, 24–25
O-ring, 33–35

P

payload specialists, 22

R

Reagan, Nancy, 16
Reagan, Ronald, 14, 16, 17
Resnik, Judith, 7, 12, 21, 23–24,
    28
Ride, Sally, 17
Rogers, William, 17

S

safety procedures, 36
Scobee, June, 22, 39
Scobee, Rich, 38
Scobee, Richard (Dick), 7, 8, 9,
    12, 20, 21, 22, *23*, 28, 30, 38,
    39, 40
Smith, Jane, 8, 10, 23
Smith, Michael, 7, 8, 9, 12, 20,
    21, 23, 30
smoke, 7, 10, 31, 33, 34